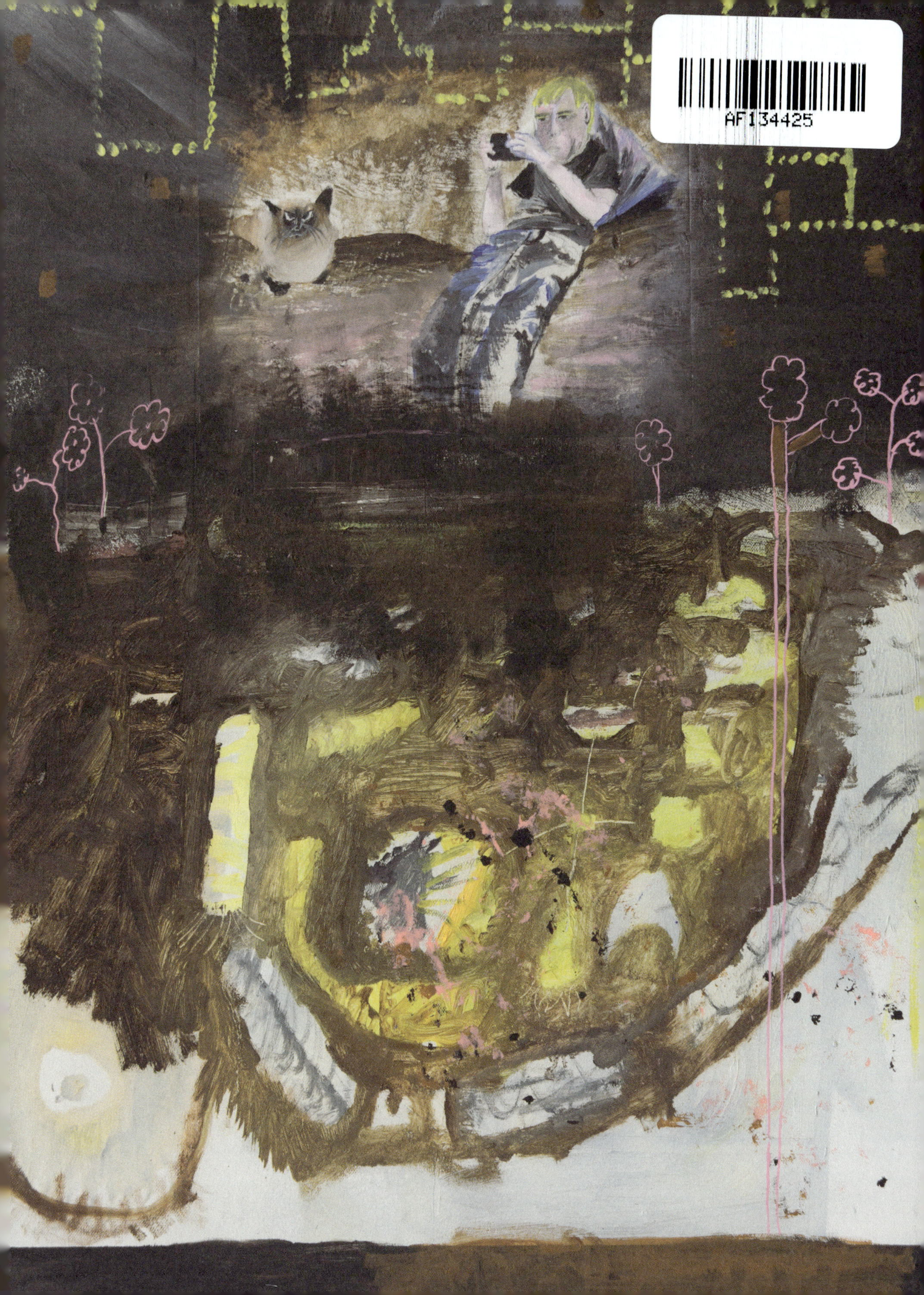

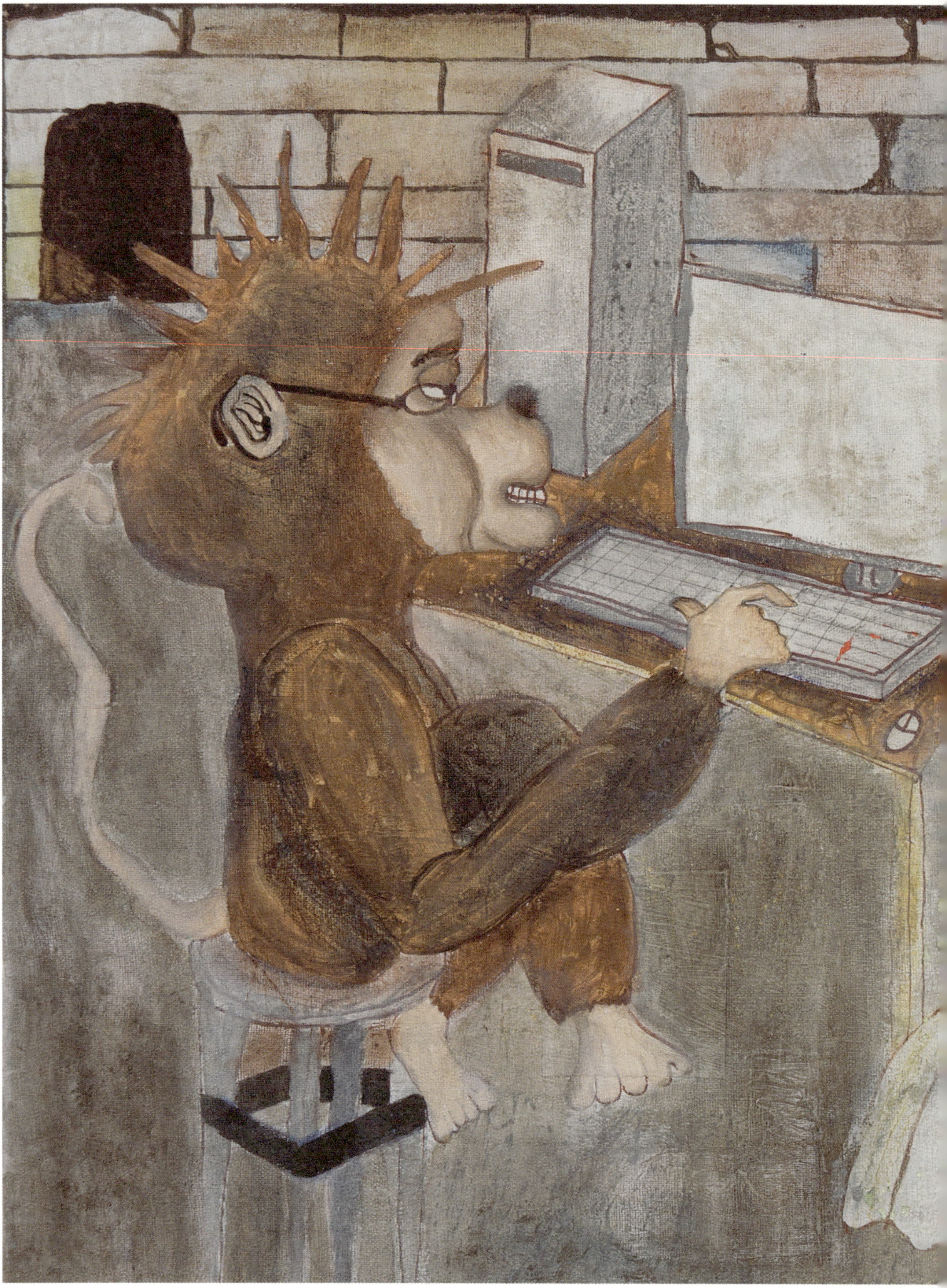

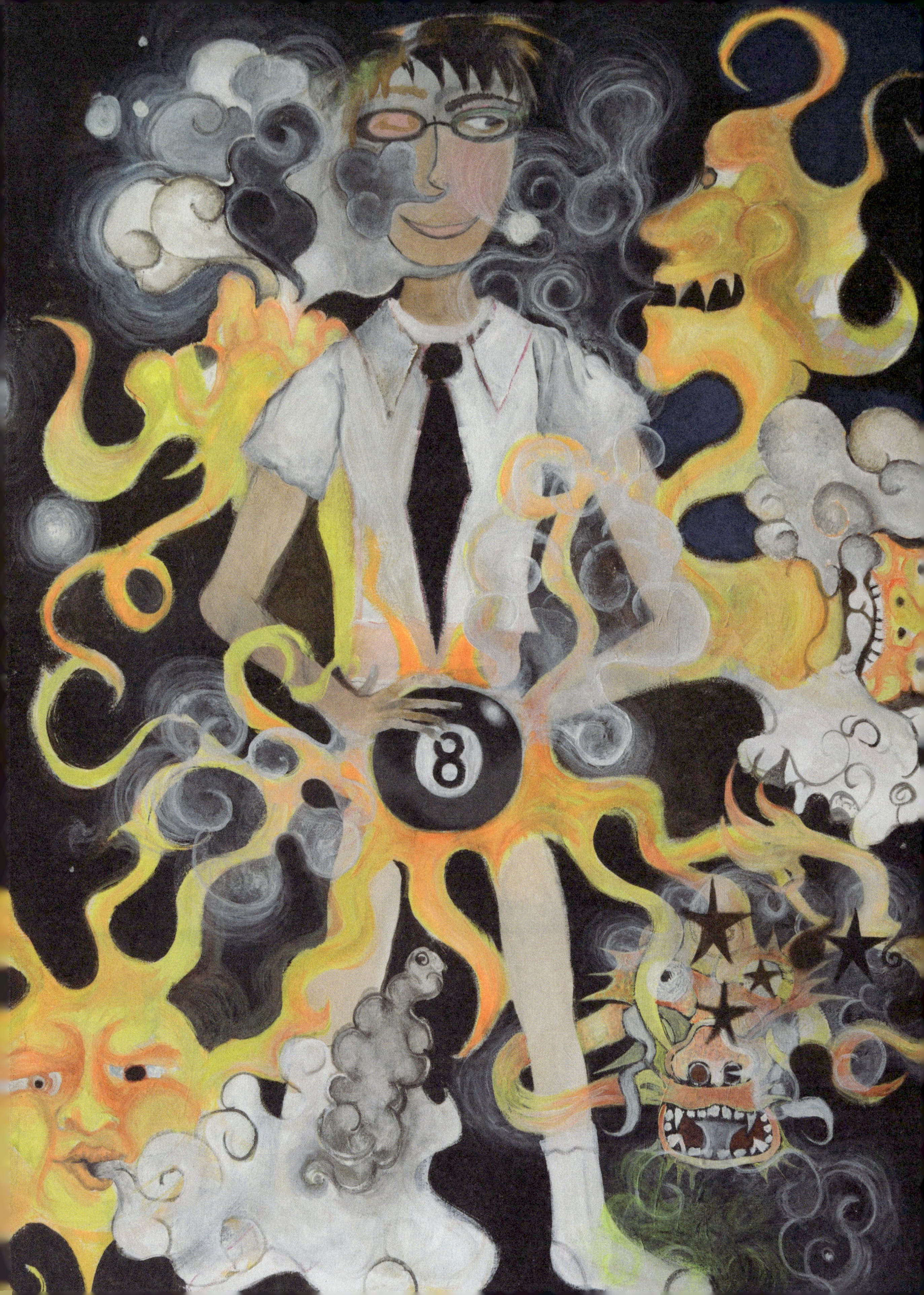

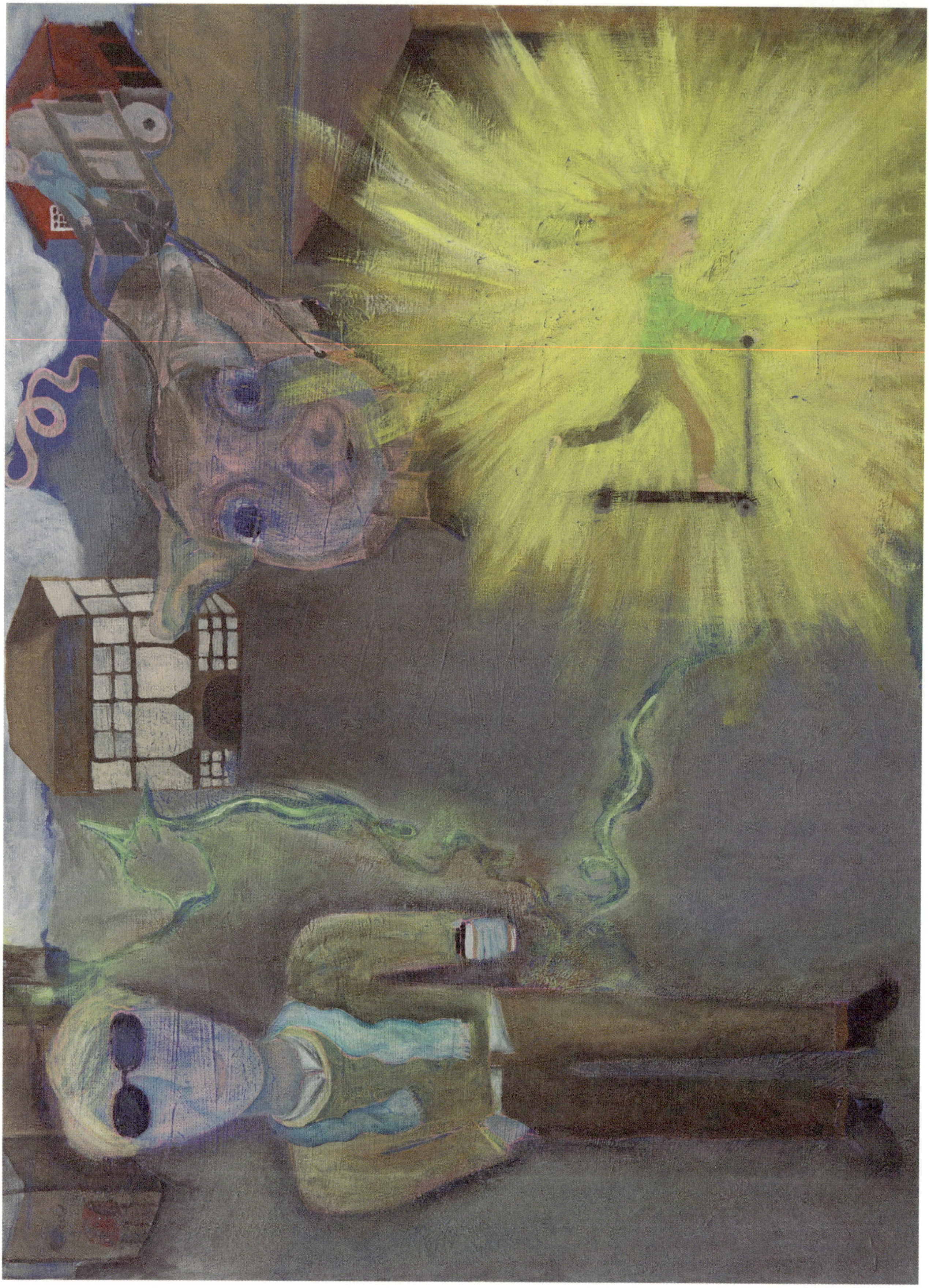

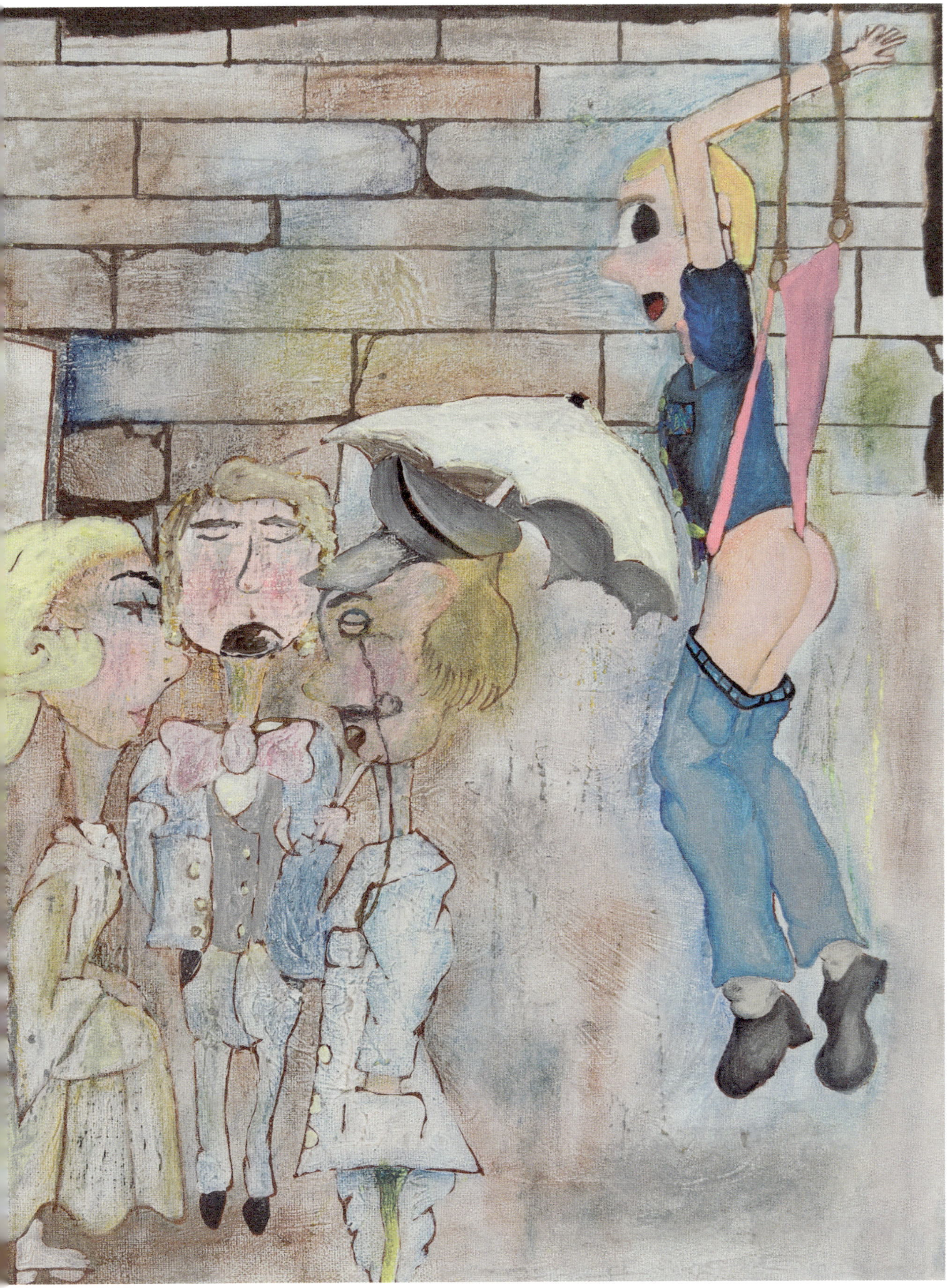

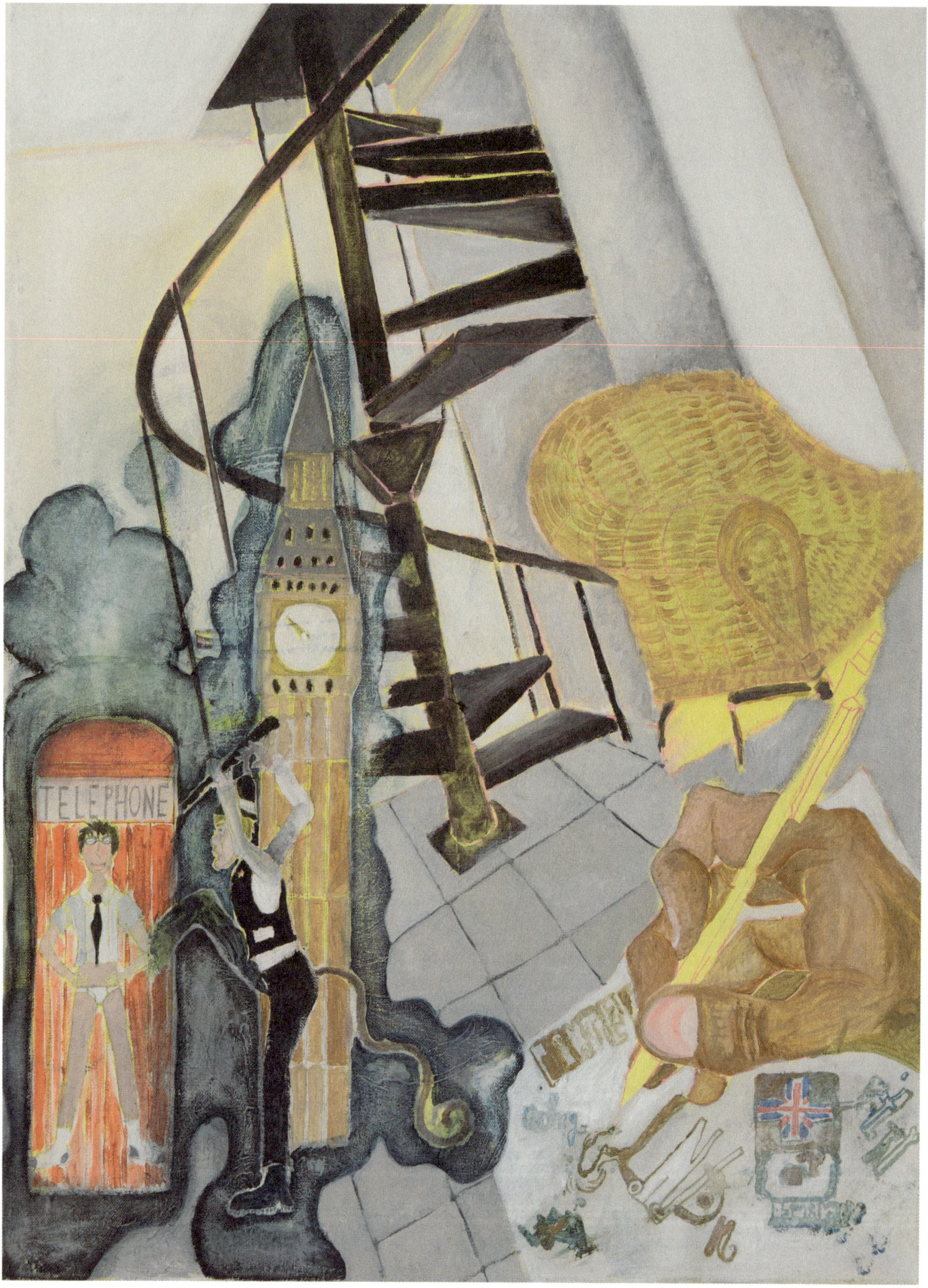
TELEPHONE

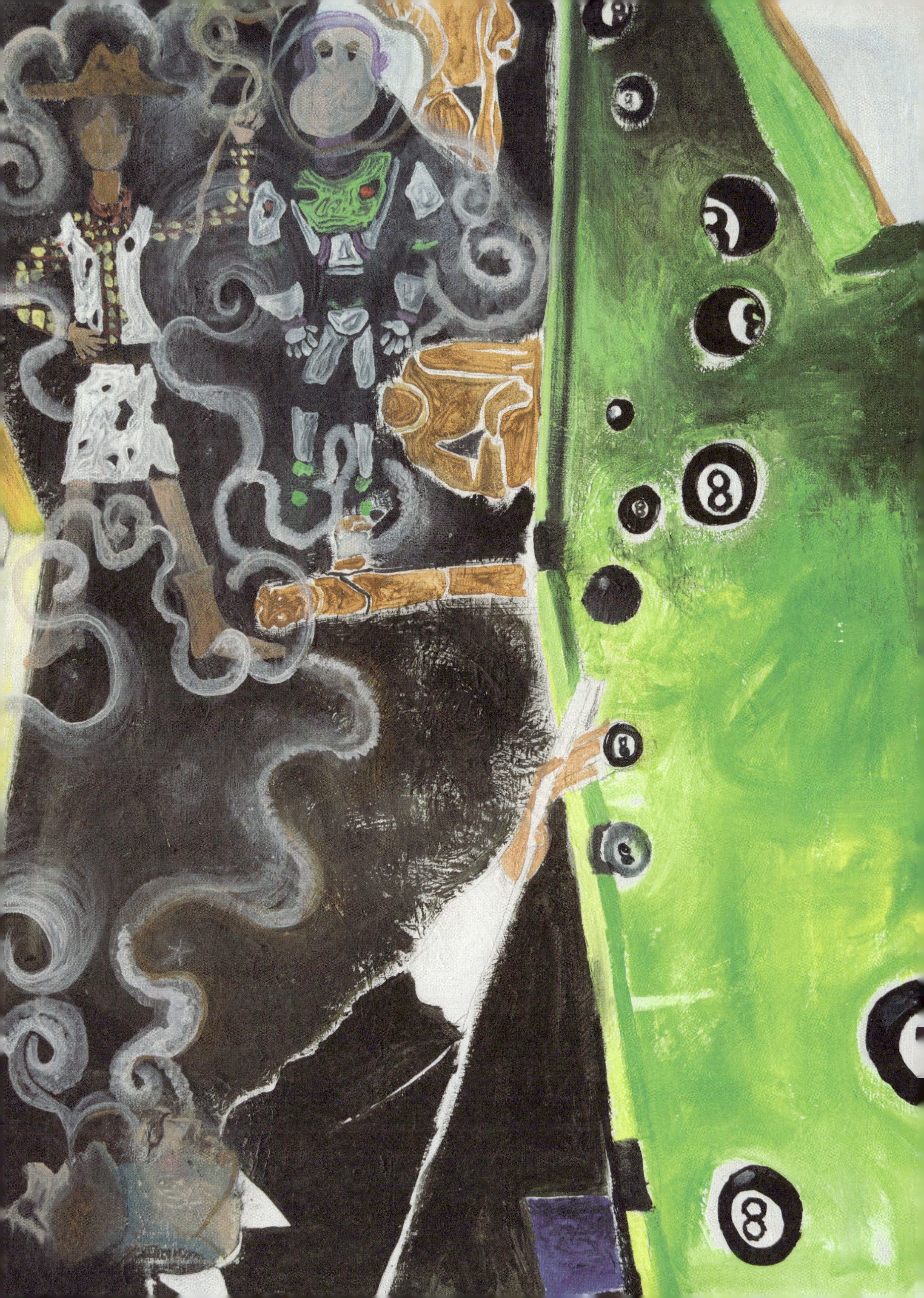

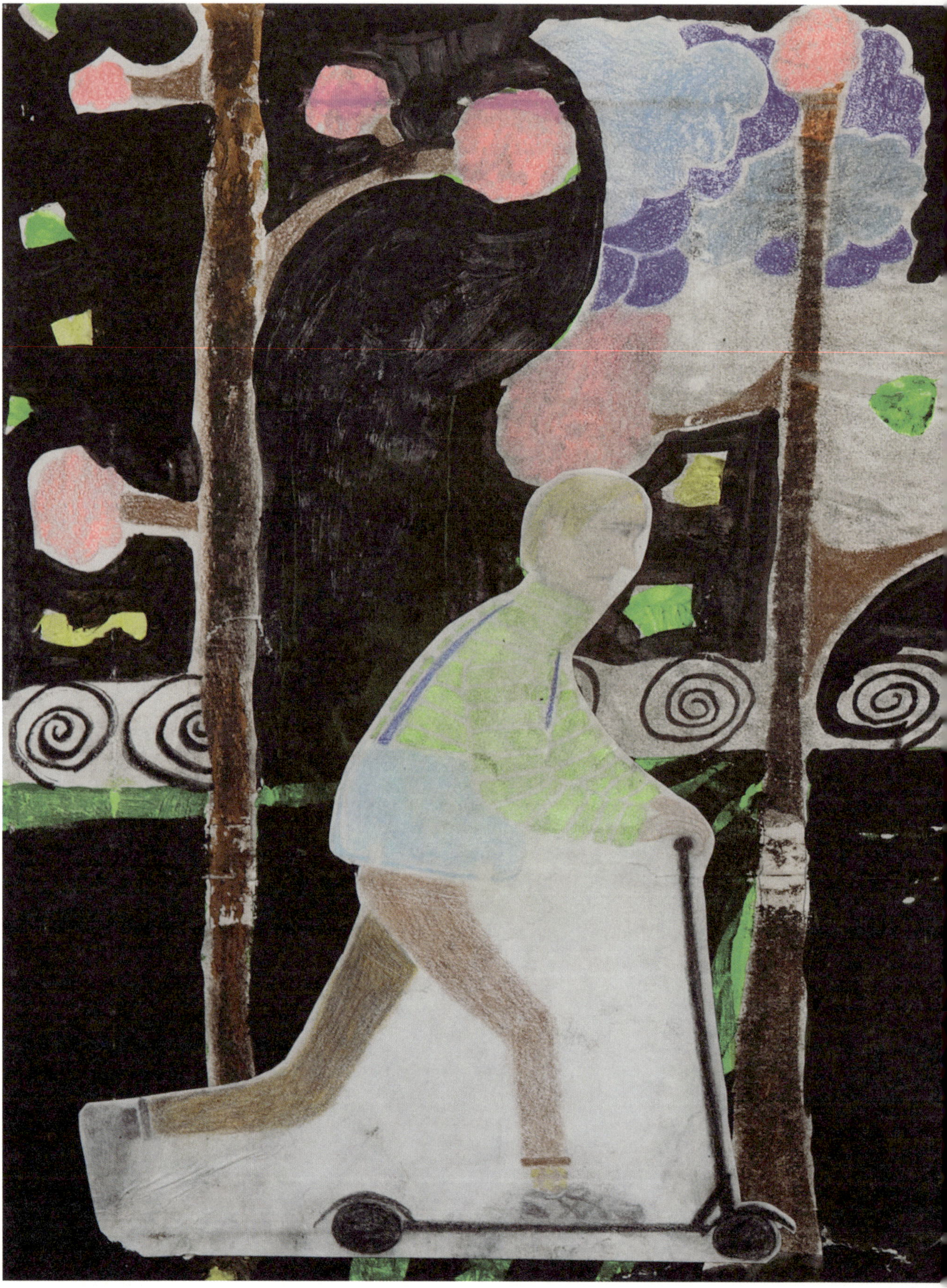

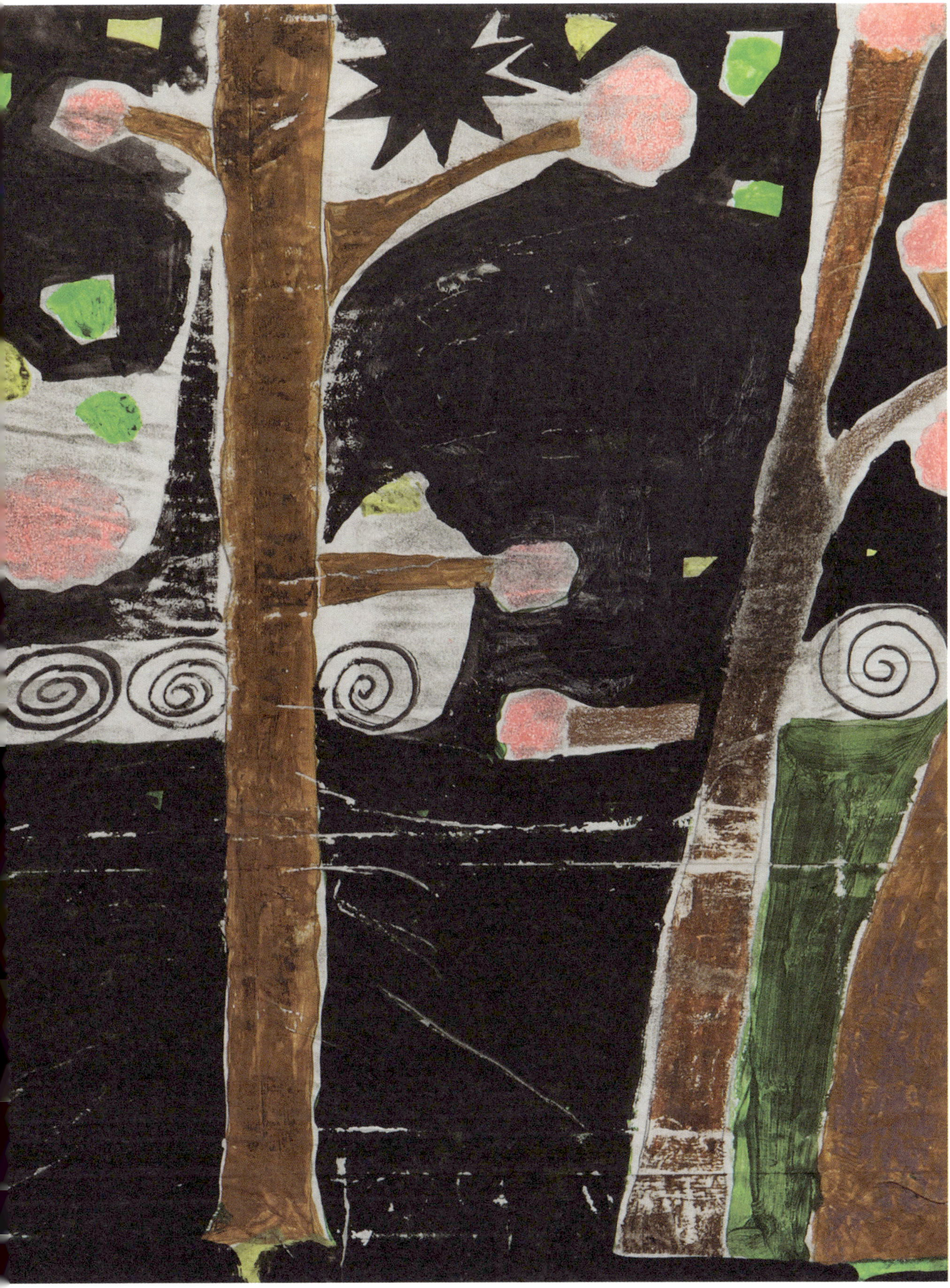

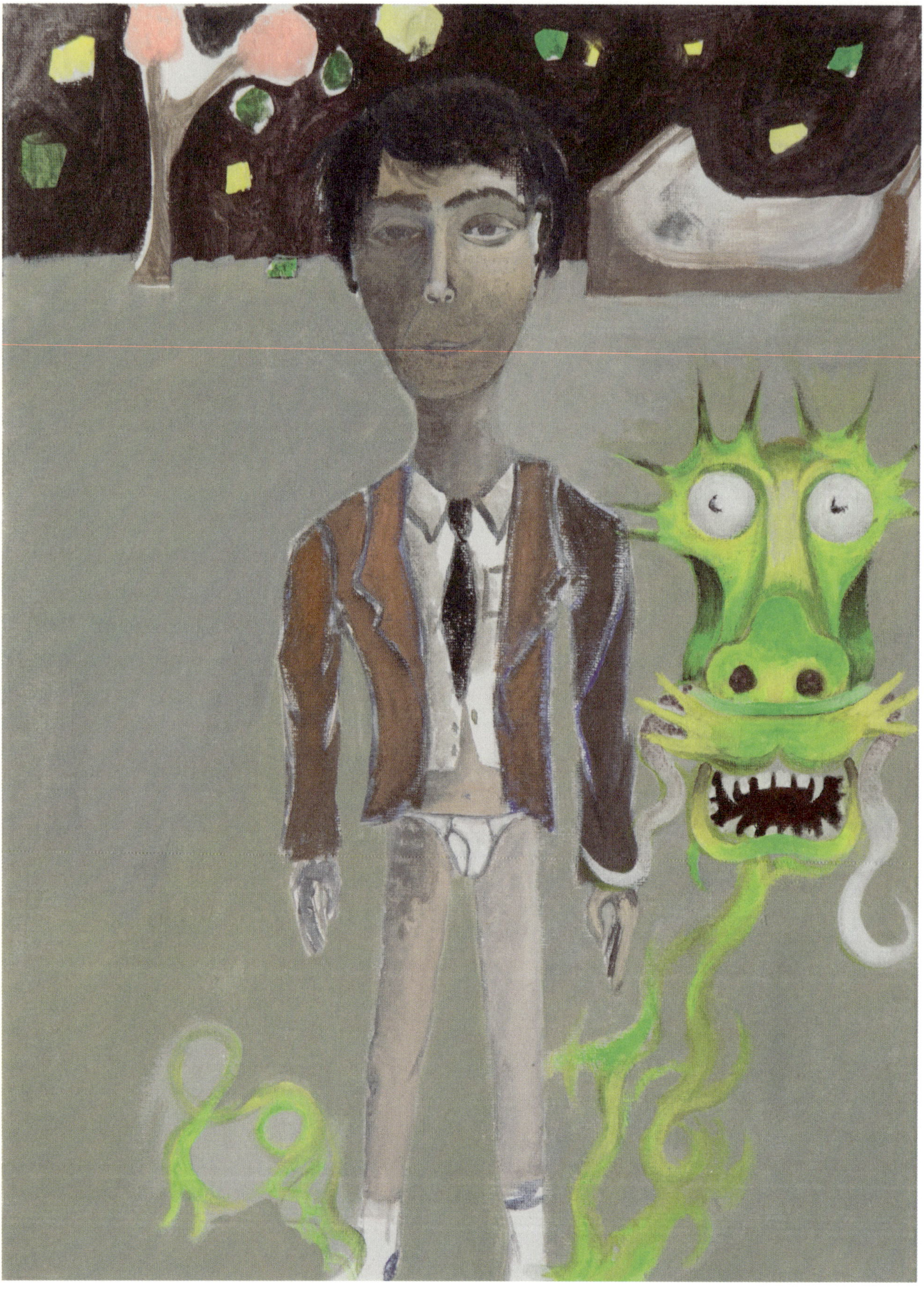

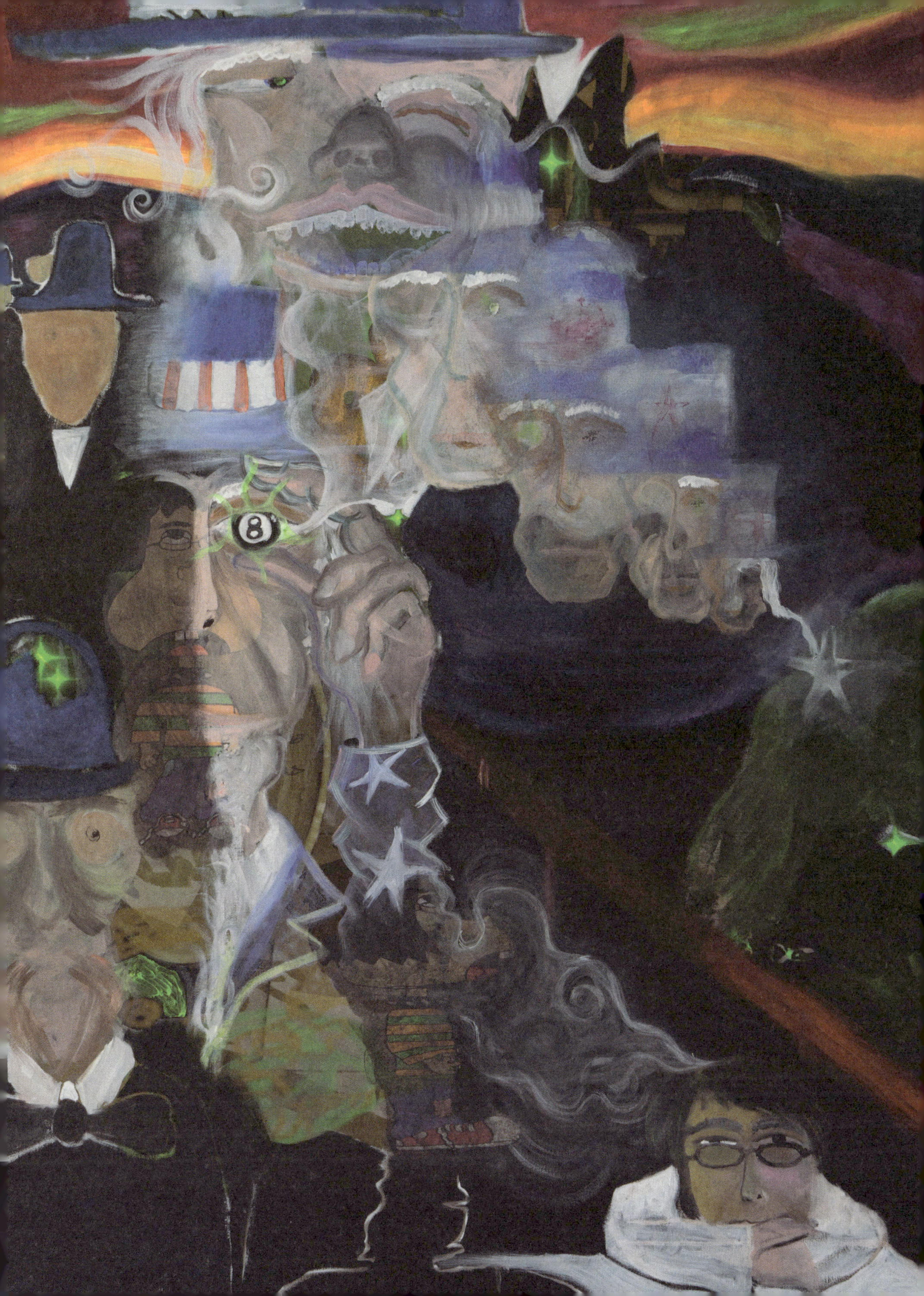

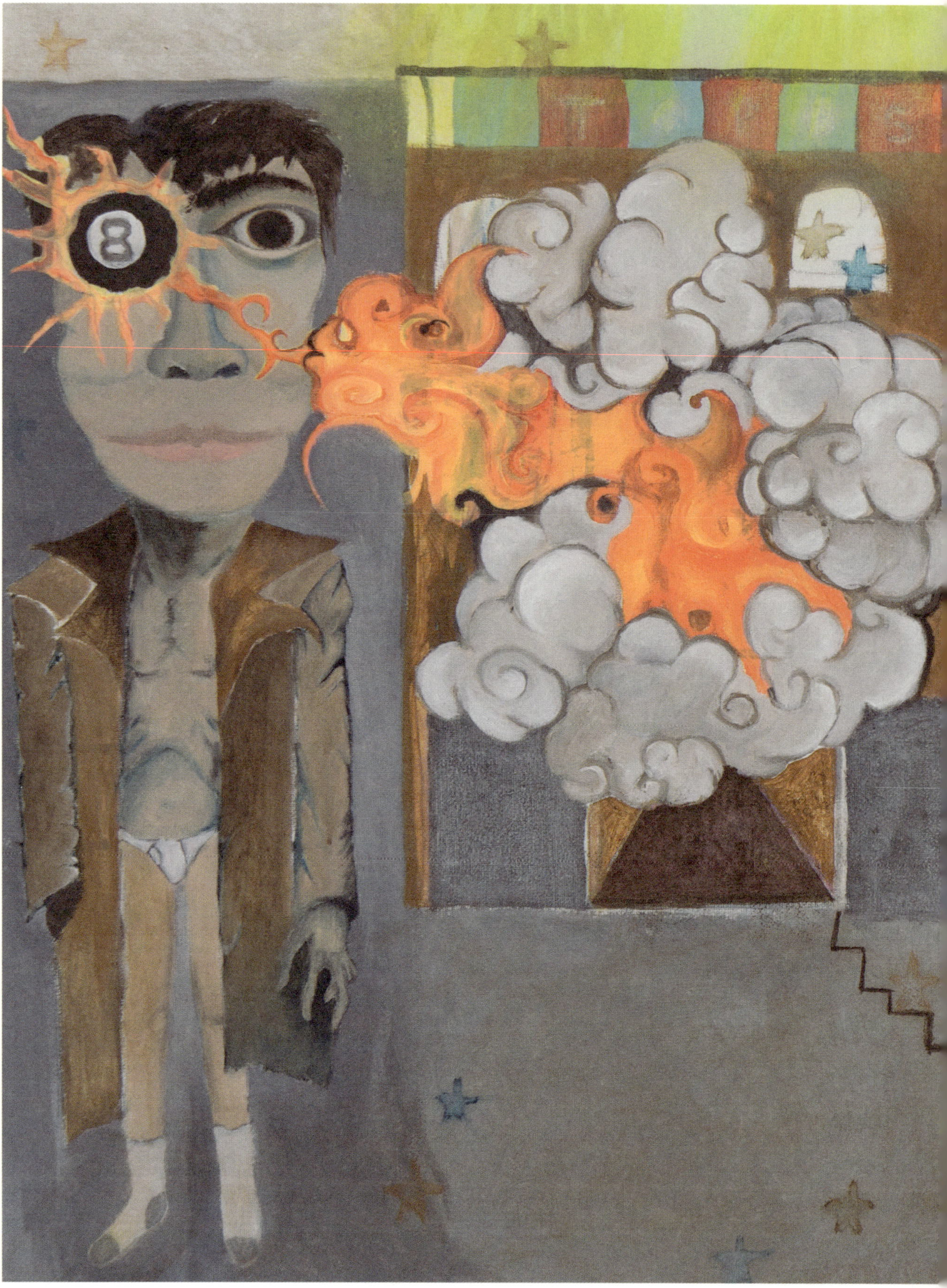

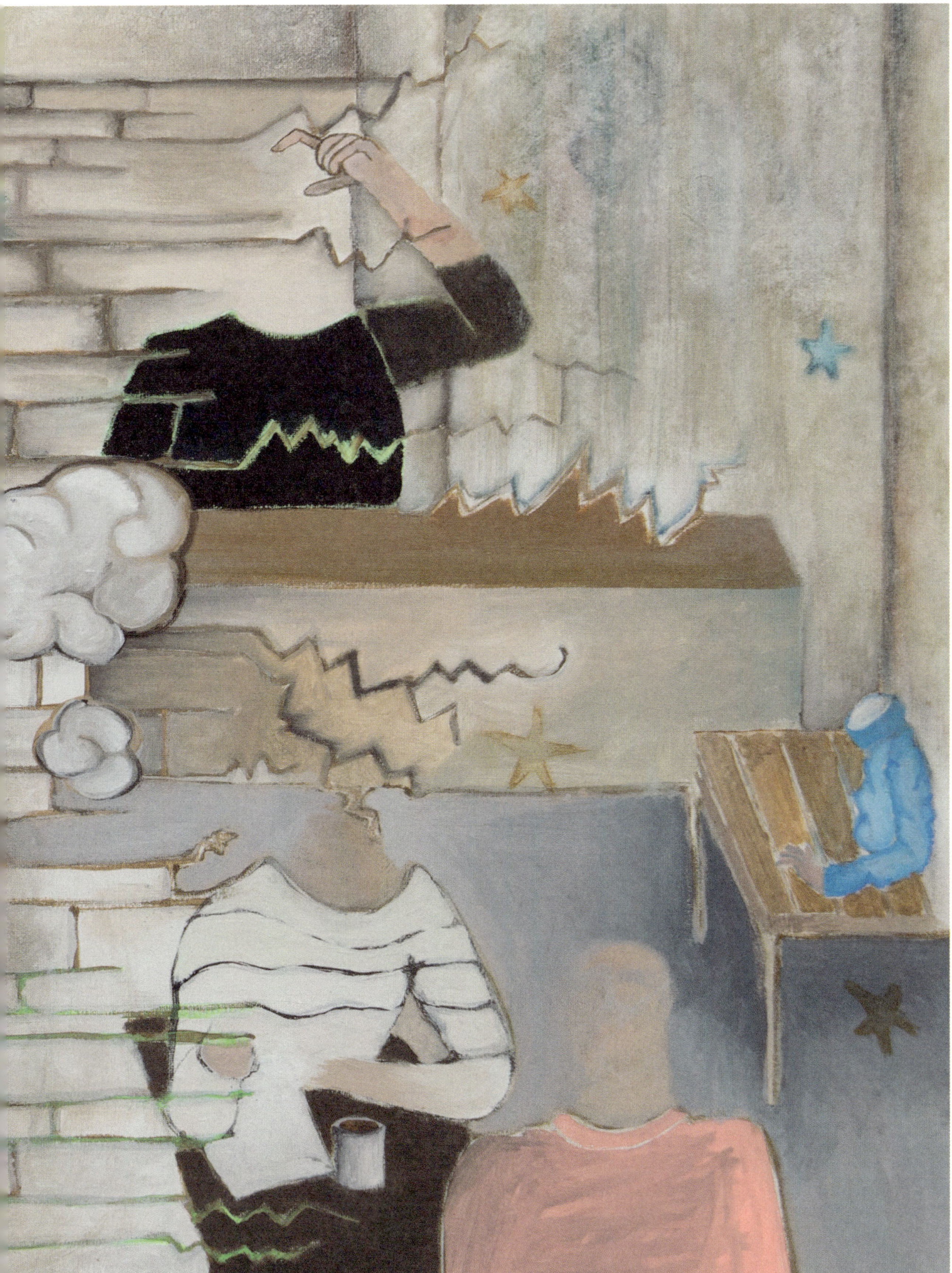

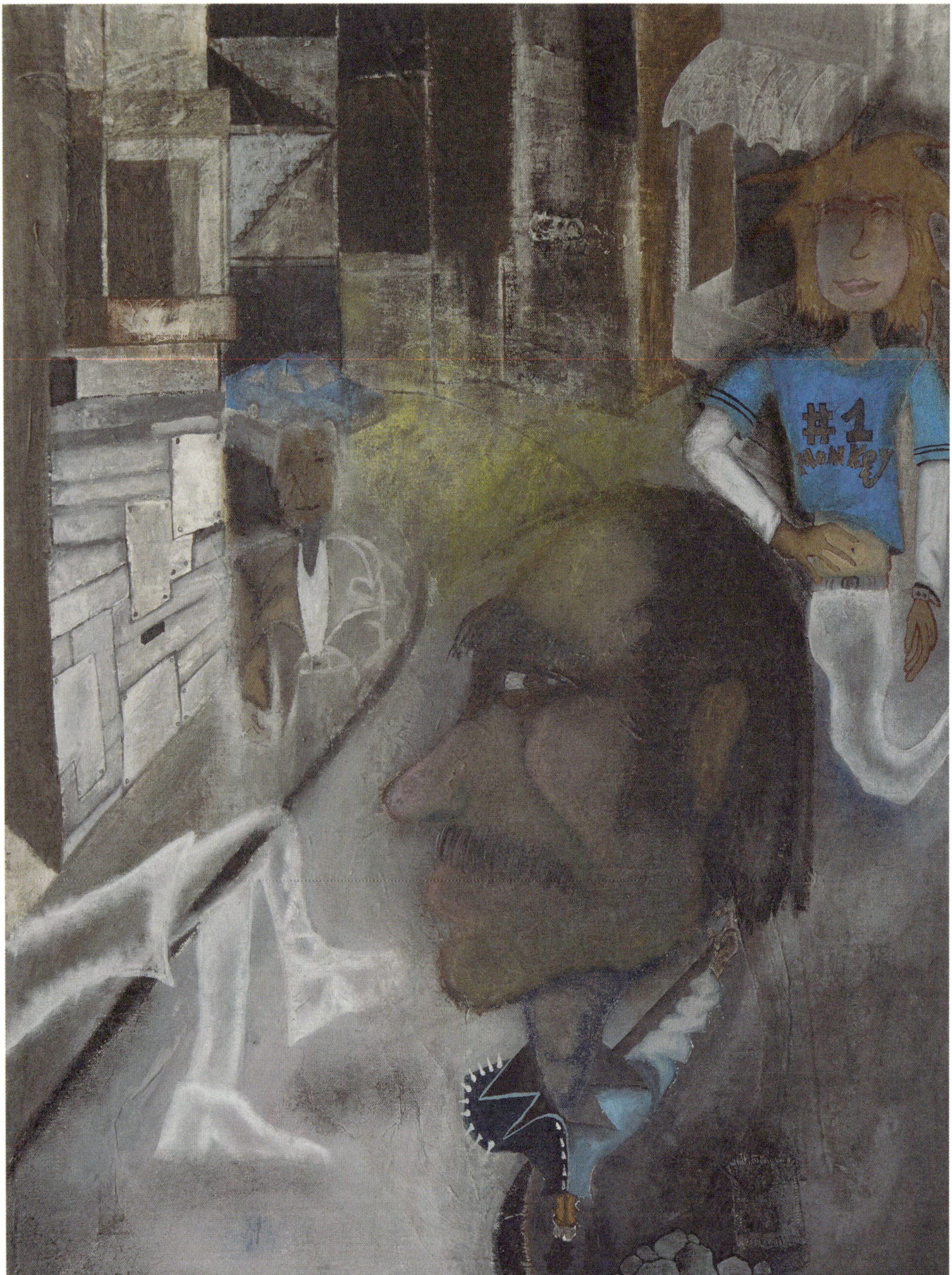
#1
MONKEY

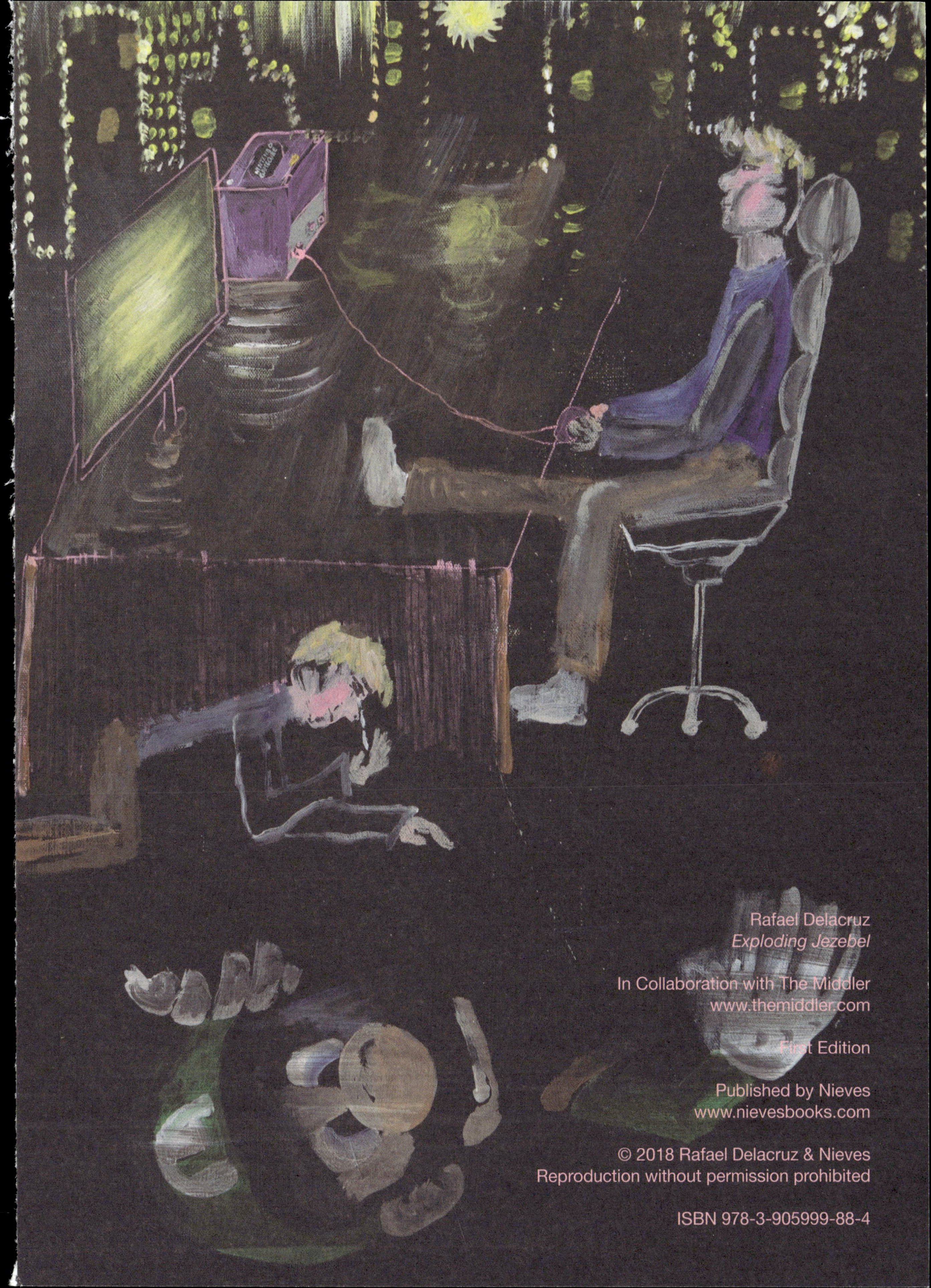

Rafael Delacruz
Exploding Jezebel

In Collaboration with The Middler
www.themiddler.com

First Edition

Published by Nieves
www.nievesbooks.com

ISBN 978-3-905999-88-4

Nieves

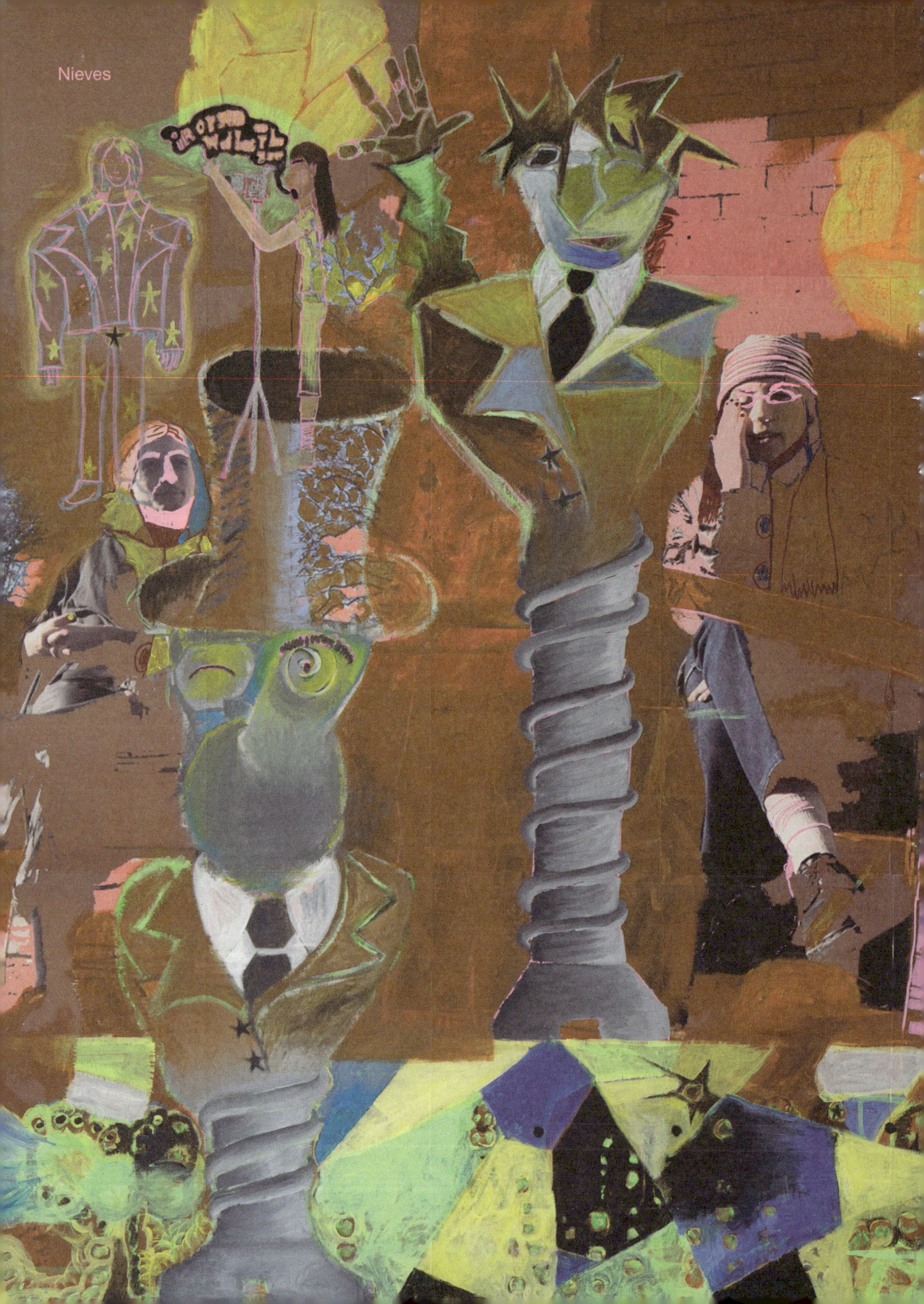